I ♥ JAPAN

BY SEITOUSHA

In this book, you will see:

Pages 3–4: *Fujisan* (Mt. Fuji), *sakura* (cherry tree), *shinkansen* (bullet train)

Pages 5–6: *matcha* (powdered green tea), *chawan* (tea bowl), *chagama* (teakettle), *hishaku* (bamboo ladle),
  chasen (tea whisk), *wagashi* (Japanese sweets)

Pages 7–8: *wagasa* (Japanese umbrella), *tanuki* (raccoon), *kitsune* (fox), *ryokucha* (green tea)

Pages 9–10: *maneki-neko* (good-fortune cat), *zabuton* (cushion)

Pages 11–12: *onigiri* (rice balls), *nori* (seaweed), *umeboshi* (pickled plum), *takuan* (pickled yellow radishes)

Pages 13–14: *kaeru* (frog), *teruteru-bouzu* (sunshine charm doll), *katatsumuri* (snail)

Pages 15–16: *tofu* (tofu), *donabe* (Japanese clay pot), *renge* (Chinese soup spoon), *negi* (green onion), *shouga* (ginger)

Pages 17–18: *mizu fusen* (water balloons)

Pages 19–20: *uchiwa* (fan), *inu* (dog)

Pages 21–22: *kanro jakushi* (ladle), *kakigori* (shaved ice), *saji* (spoon), *furin* (wind chimes)

Pages 23–24: *senko-hanabi* (sparkler), *fukuro* (owl)

Pages 25–26: *zabuton* (cushion), *inu* (dog), *chabudai* (low dining table), *ryokucha* (green tea), *kyusu* (teapot)

Pages 27–28: *kendama* (kendama cup-and-ball toys)

Pages 29–30: *te* (hand), *kagee* (making shadow puppets), *shoji* (sliding paper door)

Pages 31–32: *hyotan* (gourd), *tanuki* (raccoon), *kasa* (sedge hat), *sakazuki* (sake cup)

Pages 33–34: *daruma* (traditional Japanese dolls), *zabuton* (cushion)

Pages 35–36: *kumiame* (traditional rolled candy)

Pages 37–38: *saru* (monkey), *tenugui* (hand towel), *yuoke* (wash basin), *noren* (entrance curtain), *onsen* (hot spring bath)

Pages 39–40: *ichigo daifuku* (mochi with strawberry and sweet bean paste)

Pages 41–42: *kotatsu* (electric heating table), *neko* (cat), *mikan* (mandarin oranges), *zabuton* (cushions)

Pages 43–44: *kamakura* (igloo), *shichirin* (charcoal grill), *onna no ko* (girl), *inu* (dog)

Pages 45–46: *soba* (soba noodles), *hashi* (chopsticks), *ebi tempura* (shrimp tempura), *donburi* (bowl)

Pages 47–48: *hagoita* (battledore), *hane* (shuttlecock), *hanetsuki* (battledore and shuttlecock, a game similar
  to badminton), *saru* (monkey), *suzuri* (inkstone), *fude* (writing brush)

Gakken

Gakken Plus Co., LTD, Japan
I ♥ JAPAN
Illustrations by SEITOUSHA
Design by mill design studio
(Terumi Hara, Ayumi Hoshino)
English supervision by
Nobu Yamada, Sarah Parvis,
Dawn Teruko Laabs

ISBN 978-4-05-621070-5
Originally published in Japan as *Nihon no ehon kore naani*
by Gakken © 2015
First U.S. edition, 2018
Copyright © Gakken Plus 2018
All rights reserved.
gakkenplusna.com
10 9 8 7 6 5 4 3 2 1
PRINTED IN CHINA, MAY 2018

これ　なあに?

What is this?

ふじさん

Fujisan

Mt. Fuji

これ　なあに?

What is this?

まっちゃ

matcha

powdered green tea

これ　なあに?

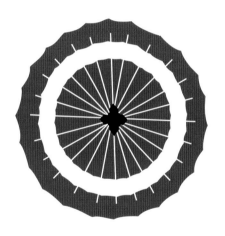

What is this?

かさ

wagasa

Japanese umbrella

これ　なあに?

What is this?

まねきねこ

maneki-neko

good-fortune cat

なかみは　なあに?

What is inside?

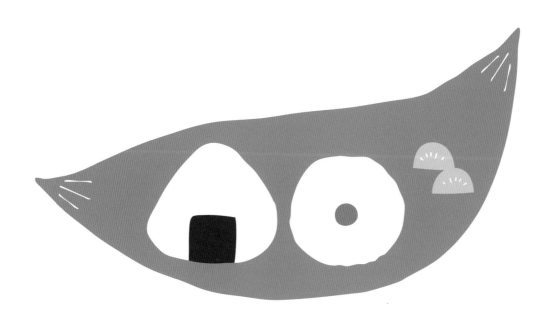

おにぎり

onigiri

rice balls

なに　みてる?

What are you looking at?

てるてる
ぼうず

teruteru-bouzu

sunshine charm doll

これ　なあに?

What is this?

とうふ

tofu

tofu

これ　なあに?

What is this?

みずふうせん

mizu fusen

water balloons

あおいの　なあに？

What is this blue thing?

うちわ

uchiwa

fan

これ　なあに?

What is this?

かきごおり

kakigori

shaved ice

これ　なあに?

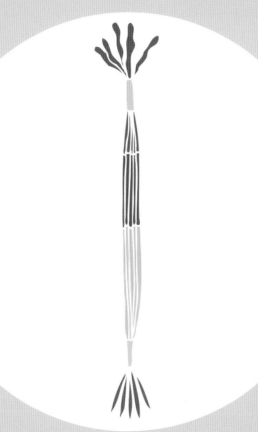

What is this?

せんこう
はなび

senko-hanabi

sparkler

あかいの　なあに?

What is this red thing?

ざぶとん

zabuton

cushion

これ　なあに?

What is this?

けんだま

kendama

kendama cup-and-ball toys

なに　してる?

What are you doing?

かげえ

kagee

making shadow puppets

これ　なあに?

What is this?

ひょうたん

hyotan

gourd

これ　なあに?

What is this?

だるま

daruma

traditional Japanese dolls

これ　なあに?

What is this?

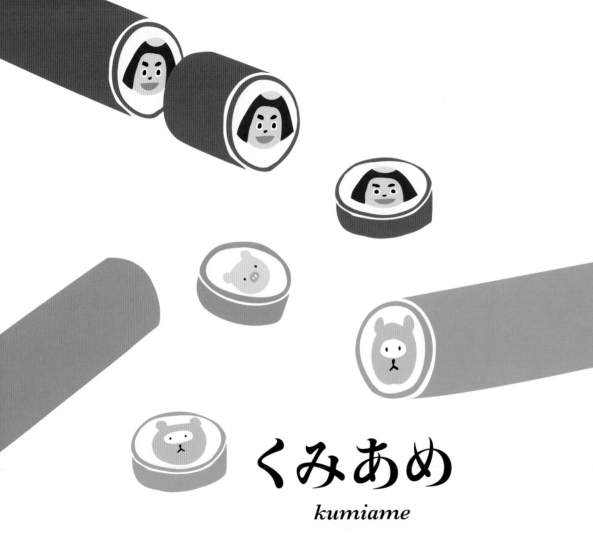

くみあめ

kumiame

traditional rolled candy

なに　するの?

What are you doing?

おんせん に はいる。

onsen ni hairu

taking a bath in a hot spring bath

これ　なあに?

What is this?

いちごだいふく

ichigo daifuku

mochi with strawberry and sweet bean paste

ふとんかな?

Is this a futon?

こたつ

kotatsu

electric heating table

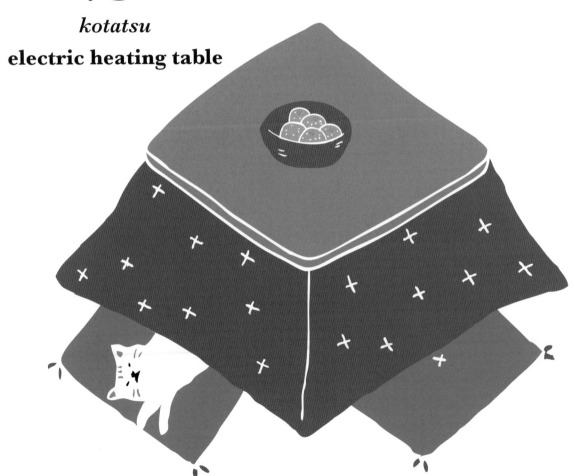

これ　なあに?

What is this?

かまくら

kamakura

igloo

これ　なあに?

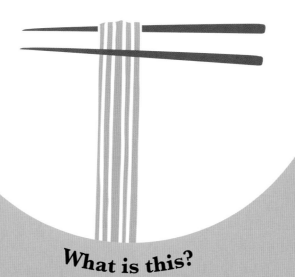

What is this?

そば

soba

soba noodles

なに　してる?

What are you doing?

はねつき

hanetsuki

**playing battledore
and shuttlecock**